D0879500

other books by Francis A. Schaeffer

Escape from Reason*
The God Who Is There*
Death in the City
Pollution and the Death of Man
The Church at the End of the 20th Century
The Mark of the Christian
The Church before the Watching World
He Is There and He Is Not Silent*
True Spirituality
Genesis in Space and Time
The New Super-Spirituality
Basic Bible Studies
Art and the Bible
No Little People
Two Contents, Two Realities
Everybody Can Know (Francis & Edith Schaeffer)
No Final Conflict
Joshua and the Flow of Biblical History*
How Should We Then Live?

*Group study guide available

back to freedom and dignity
francis a. schaeffer

inter-varsity press
downers grove, illinois 60515

Fifth printing,
July 1977

InterVarsity Press is
the book publishing
division of Inter-Varsity
Christian Fellowship.

ISBN 0-87784-439-9

Printed in the United
States of America

foreword

"The universe was not pregnant with life nor the biosphere with man. Our number came up in the Monte Carlo games"—Jacques Monod.

"To man qua man we readily say good riddance"—B. F. Skinner.

Born by chance. Dead by design. Is this the beginning and end of man? If we are to believe two eminent scientists—yes.

Dr. Francis A. Schaeffer, however, believes we needn't be so pessimistic. The truth lies elsewhere—in the Christian view of man.

In the present book, Dr. Schaeffer extends the argument he first presented in chapters six and seven of The Church at the End of the 20th Century, *where he emphasized the pressures on society that open the way for modern forms of human manipulation. There he was ahead of time in what he was telling us. Here he shows how rapidly the techniques of manipulation have been developing since that book was published. For readers who wish to pursue the subject further and to come to grips with the Christian option, we especially recommend three of Dr. Schaeffer's earlier books—*The God Who Is There, He Is There and He Is Not Silent *and* Death in the City.

The Publisher

. . . Lord . . .
thou didst create all things,
and by thy will they existed and were created.
(Revelation 4:11)

So God created man in his own image, in the image of God
he created him; male and female he created them.
(Genesis 1:27)

But now thus says the LORD,
he who created you, O Jacob,
he who formed you, O Israel:
"Fear not, for I have redeemed you;
I have called you by name, you are mine.
When you pass through the waters I will be with you;
and through the rivers, they shall not overwhelm you;
when you walk through fire you shall not be burned,
and the flame shall not consume you.
For I am the LORD your God,
the Holy One of Israel, your Savior."
(Isaiah 43:1-3)

**back to
freedom
and
dignity**

In the early months of 1971 the general public began to feel the first shock waves of the biological bomb which has recently exploded in scientific circles. Before that only those scientists and intellectuals who were up on the latest developments in molecular physics, biochemistry and genetics knew what was happening. Only they had any indication of the implications for future society. But now popular journals in Europe and the United States are carrying news story after news story on the revolution in the life sciences, a revolution which is raising questions for human society that were previously dreamed of only by science fiction writers and professional futurologists.

The major challenge is how to handle the recently developed techniques of human engineering and human manipulation. It is important for Christians to pay close attention to the course of events associated with these developments. We are going to be called upon to answer questions we have never considered before, and we should be prepared to respond. First we need to understand from the Christian viewpoint what is happening. More important, we must help those in decision-making capacities to recognize the implications of the issues we face together as a human race.

In short, Christians should prepare to take the lead in giving direction to cultural change. And if it goes poorly, as well it might in the post-Christian world, then we should be consciously preparing the next generation for the new battles it will face.

What in fact are we facing in the way of technological change? And what kind of moral and religious issues are raised by these new developments?

To answer these questions, I will refer to a series of articles, all but one of which have appeared in the mass media and have thus been available to the American populace. I will begin with two items, one of which appeared in the *New York Times* in March 1971, the other in *Newsweek* a month later. I will end with an item appearing in *Time* in September 1971. A close analysis of articles from this short six-month period will give us a reading on the shock waves of the biological bomb, genetic engineering and manipulation by chemistry and electricity.

jacques monod: chance and necessity

The first two news releases focus on Jacques Monod, the French molecular biologist who, along with two other French scientists, won the Nobel prize in 1965 for discovering the replication mechanism of genetic material and the manner in which cells synthesize protein. Soon after his book, *Le Hazard et la*

Nécessité, was published in France in 1970, Jacques Monod again came to the attention of newsmen, for the French edition, as *Newsweek* put it, "unexpectedly zoomed onto the Parisian best-seller list just behind the French translation of Eric Segal's 'Love Story.' " By March 1971, some 155,000 copies were in print. In the fall of 1971, Alfred A. Knopf released the book in its English translation, *Chance and Necessity.* But long before the English-speaking public had a translation available to them, the mass media had carried articles summarizing the major thrust of Monod's latest thinking. One of those articles was written by John C. Hess and appeared in the *New York Times* (March 15, 1971), page 6; another in *Newsweek* (April 26, 1971), page 99.

Monod's argument in *Chance and Necessity* is highly sophisticated and relies a great deal on data and judgment concerning molecular structure and cell structure. Nonetheless, the primary thrust of his book is not scientific but philosophic. Much of what he says is based not so much on his scientific investigation as on his philosophic, and one might say religious, presuppositions. *Newsweek* summarizes it as follows:

> After some 30 years of research in biochemistry and genetics, the short, trim scientist is convinced that man's existence is due to the chance collision between miniscule particles of nucleic acid and proteins in the vast "pre-biotic soup." Indeed, Monod argues that all life results from interaction of pure chance—unpredictable mutations—and necessity, or Darwinian selection.

But let us listen to what Monod himself says:

> . . . Chance *alone* is at the source of every innovation, of all creation in the biosphere. Pure chance, absolutely free but blind, at the very root of the stupendous edifice of evolution: this central concept of modern biol-

11

ogy is no longer one among other possible or even conceivable hypotheses. It is today the *sole* conceivable hypothesis, the only one that squares with observed and tested fact. And nothing warrants the supposition—or the hope—that on this score our position is likely ever to be revised. (*Chance and Necessity*, pp. 112-113)

This radical position stands as the basis of Monod's entire view of reality. A man's categories, his basic views of life, rest on his concept of origin. Monod assumes that the only thinkable position is that man is the result of the impersonal plus time plus chance. With such a position, there is nothing in the universe itself to which man can appeal in regard to values. Man, whoever he is, is alone. Monod writes:

If he accepts this message—accepts all it contains—then man must at last wake out of his millenary dream; and in doing so, wake to his total solitude, his fundamental isolation. Now does he at last realize that, like a gypsy, he lives on the boundary of an alien world. A world that is deaf to his music, just as indifferent to his hopes as it is to his suffering or his crimes. (pp. 172-173)

Elsewhere, along the same line he writes:

The universe was not pregnant with life nor the biosphere with man. Our number came up in a Monte Carlo game. Is it any wonder if, like the person who has just made a million at the casino, we feel strange and a little unreal? (pp. 145-146)

How, then, if man lives in such a universe shall he decide how to live? Where will he get his moral principles? If there are no moral absolutes against which man can measure his actions, how then shall he understand what value is?

In *Chance and Necessity* (pp. 166-180) Monod attempts to construct an ethic of knowledge based on scientific objectivity. He tries to wed knowledge and value by declaring that man must make a choice (an ethical choice) to accept whatever results from an objective consideration of the facts which lie before him. From this ethical choice of a primary value, knowledge starts (p. 176).

Since there is a call here to objective knowledge as a norm, it would appear that Monod is claiming that *what is* and *what ought to be* are one. But the interview with Monod which Hess reports in the *New York Times* shows that this is not the case:

"One of the great problems of philosophy," he [Monod] went on, "is the relationship between the realm of knowledge and the realm of values. Knowledge is what is, values are what ought to be. I would say that all traditional philosophies up to and including Marxism have tried to derive the 'ought' from the 'is.'

"Now my point of view is that this is impossible, this is a farce. You cannot derive any sort of 'ought' from the 'is.' If it is true that there is no intention in the universe and if it is true that man as any other animal species is a pure accident in evolution, it might just as well not have appeared.

"If this is so, then we cannot derive any 'ought' from the 'is,' and our system of values is free for us to choose. In fact, we must choose a system of values. We cannot live without it: We cannot live personally, we cannot deal with society." . . .

Mr. Monod said that he drew his own system of values from the existential ethics of his friend the late Albert Camus—"an ethics based on a free choice." He said the key to his book lay in the quotation from Camus on the dedication page. Describing the mythical struggle of Sisyphus to push the stone to the mountain-top, only to have it roll to the bottom, in a mystery no longer to be ascribed to the punishment of the gods, Camus writes:

"This universe, from now on without a master, seems to him neither sterile nor futile. The struggle toward the summits itself is enough to fill the heart of man."

It is clear, therefore, that Monod is not claiming objectivity for the value he has chosen to place on objective knowledge. This value resides in a prior choice that Monod has made, and thus it is totally man-centered, even one-man-centered. Essentially Monod's ethic, as all existential ethics tend to be, is solipsistic.

Monod concludes *Chance and Necessity* with this:

The ancient covenant [between man and the universe] is in pieces; man knows at last that he is alone in the universe's unfeeling immensity, out of which he emerged only by chance. His destiny is nowhere spelled out, nor is his duty. The kingdom above or the darkness below: it is for him to choose. (p. 180)

What sorts of values will man then choose? And how shall he choose them? One thing is clear: If man sees himself as Monod sees him, the values are up for grabs. Anything can become a value. Furthermore, men will have no reason not to use the modern forms of manipulation in order to achieve their purposes and implement their arbitrary values. When Alfred E. Kinsey studied the sexual behavior of contemporary men, the primary effect of his report was to suggest that whatever was the average behavior of people of any culture was right. In sexual matters, this is the way Sweden operates today. With modern means of accumulating data, such sociological norms are eminently practicable. Marshall McLuhan, for example, emphasizes this when he says that democracy is finished, that we are living in a global village. There may eventually be gigantic computers which will record what people think and what people are doing at any one given moment, and this will become the law of the world.

The only other workable possibility for moral values on a large sociological scale is the development of an elite. It is in this direction that Jacques Monod himself seems to lean, at least when he is talking about the future of man. Hess quotes Monod as follows:

> "In my opinion," he [Monod] said, "the future of mankind is going to be decided within the next two generations, and there are two absolute requisites: We must aim at a stable-state society and the destruction of nuclear stock piles."
>
> A stable-state society, he explained, would be one with a very limited growth in population and even, perhaps, in technology. To achieve it, he said, will call for "some form of world authority."
>
> "Otherwise," he continued, "I don't see how we can survive much later than 2050."

When we hear such language as this, a little bell ought to ring. Here is another voice with authority calling for the development of an elite that will set up arbitrary values, arbitrary absolutes whereby to control the world. Even if the goals are at first sight laudable—the salvation of the human race—the implications for human freedom are there for all of us to see. The problem is that with man being considered a product of the impersonal plus time plus chance, all values are open to manipulation.

What a tragedy that such a system should come from Jacques Monod himself, for Monod's grandfather was one of the greatest evangelical preachers in France! **15**

Something happened, I don't know what, and friends who know the family don't know either, but somehow Monod's heart and mind were turned against Christ and Christianity, and here is the result. It is a fact to weep over and something to keep in mind as we ourselves present Christ to our children.

francis crick: why I study biology

The next item I would like to discuss is a speech made by Dr. Francis Crick in St. Louis in March 1971. Dr. Crick is the scientist who, along with Dr. James D. Watson, unravelled the DNA code. He is considered one of the most outstanding men in the area of biology today. But Francis Crick is an atheist; he hates Christianity and would do anything to destroy it.

Crick has written two books, *The Origin of the Genetic Code* and *Of Molecules and Men.* Here, however, I want to refer to a lecture which he gave to a select group of scientists. In this lecture, entitled "Why I Study Biology," he says flatly what he feels motivates him:

It is difficult to say it [my motivation] in a few words. If you had to find a simple description of why I do biological research, it is for philosophical and what you might call religious reasons.

Crick admits that he is not doing biology for the sake of pure science. A crucial part of the view of life that Francis Crick expounds, as we can clearly see from what he writes, is the idea that man can be essentially reduced to the chemical and physical properties that go to make up the DNA template. That's all man is.

Philosophically, therefore, Francis Crick is a reductionist, that is, one who would reduce man from a complex personal being made in the image of God to simply an electro-chemical machine. Unfortunately, such a notion not only makes man junk but soon leads to the idea that man can and just as well may be manipulated with impunity.

In his lecture he goes further and mentions the fact that, when he was in California visiting a university, he met a charming girl who asked him about his birthday and talked to him about astrology and the age of Aquarius. He also noted that the bookstores were heavily stocked with books on the occult. Here is his reaction:

> I think one has to say that scientifically, astrology really is complete nonsense. I have tried very hard to think of a way in which it could make some sense and it's too much. I wonder whether people who feel that way should be at a university.

Crick's statement is really a threat. Who, then, is going to be allowed in the universities in this new world? Of course, as Christians we reject astrology and the concept of the age of Aquarius. To this extent we agree with Francis Crick concerning the content of these. But what he is suggesting is not just that the content of astrology is wrong, but that people should be shut away from university opportunities simply on the basis of what they believe. I think he would say the same thing about Bible-believing Christians. There will be no place for Christian students in the university if this kind of man takes over the elite. The doors will be shut.

Francis Crick continues:

> The major conclusion which one draws from present day biology is the importance of natural selection. The essence of natural selection, and this is the thing that people find very hard to accept, is that it's motivated by chance events. It is not pre-programmed but is driven by chance events. You can make an argument that chance is the only real source of true novelty.

In other words, he is agreeing with Jacques Monod. Natural selection is not programmed; it is generated by chance. A little further on in his speech, however, Dr. Crick says, "You cannot lay down a general trend [for the course of evolution]; natural selection is cleverer than that. It will think of combinations and ways of doing things which haven't been foreseen." The language here is interesting because it attributes to natural selection a sort of personality. In *The Origin of the Genetic Code* (1968) Crick begins to spell Nature with a capital about halfway through the book, and in *Of Molecules and Men* (1967) he calls nature a "she." In other words, he personalizes what by definition is impersonal according to his own system. Why? Because he can't stand the implications of impersonality, and because this kind of semantic mysticism gives relief to people caught in the web of the impersonal.

We must be careful of such a tricky use of language. By his own definition Crick lives in an impersonal universe, but by the connotation of the language he uses, Crick personalizes the impersonal universe and calls natural selection "clever." Such language takes the pressure off and all of a sudden people fail to understand what they have read.

Perhaps if people today were to take good reading courses, they would be better off. Americans don't read enough (that's true), and Americans read too much (that's true too). What I mean is that many don't read enough material to really be informed, and yet they read too much because what they do read they often do not stop to assimilate and think through. They whiz through it and get what I call a first-order experience, a sort of mystical feeling, not a genuine understanding. I urge you, with all my soul, in such a day as ours to really, truly learn to read!

For practice in reading to see what really is being

said, we don't have to look any further than *Newsweek, Time, Life* and the *New York Times.* If we learn to read even these, we can understand a good deal of what is coming and what may help us to protect the children we are rearing. And if we in turn can teach them to read these magazines and understand what they are reading, it will help, for much of what they report relates directly to men's religious orientation and shows the orientation of the present "liberal mind."

Francis Crick, for example, says that his scientific enterprise is governed by a basic religious stance. And while he recognizes that the particular stance he takes is anti-religious in conventional terms, "it is a religious attitude because it's concerned with religious problems." He is absolutely right. What Crick and other scientists are doing is bringing forth a religion based on science.

Later in his lecture, Dr. Crick turns to the area of mental behavior and how it is determined. He says, "We'd like to know more about mental health—how much is genetically determined and how much depends on the environment." Is it not clear, here, how man suddenly disappears? There are only two factors: (1) heredity and (2) environment. Is it 90 of one and 10 of the other? Or 10 of one and 90 of the other? It makes no difference. Either factor or both together are no more than mechanical. In your stream of consciousness, if you think in psychological terms, the person isn't there. Again man is made up of only these mechanical factors. This will become even clearer as we analyze B. F. Skinner's views, but here, too, it isn't just that God is dead; man is dead as well, because he becomes simply the product of the original impersonal with only the addition of the equally impersonal time and chance. He is a flow of consciousness. He has a genetic code. He has an environment which influences that which comes as a product of the genetic code. That's all he is and has. Man is dead indeed.

The last section of Dr. Crick's lecture really brought me up short, for he says explicitly what with those who press genetic engineering was implicit all along but generally lay hidden beneath the surface. Now he says it openly. I'm referring here to his discussion of the biological bomb and the relationship between biology and politics. What is the state to do about biology? Dr. Crick tells us:

Nonetheless, you must realize that much of the political thinking of this country [the United States] is very difficult to justify biologically. It was valid to say, in the period of the American Revolution, when people were oppressed by priests and kings, that all men were created equal. But it doesn't have biological validity. It may have some mystical validity in a religious context, but when you ask what you mean by all people being created equal, it is not the same as saying that they should all have equal opportunity. It's not only biologically not true, it's also biologically undesirable. If you had a population in which everybody was the same, any biologist would say that it was a very bad situation, that it was too homogeneous. You must have variety in biological situations. Yet, this is not the sort of thing that is regarded as particularly tactful to say. But sooner or later people have got to be saying these things. We all know, I think, or are beginning to realize, that the future is in our own hands, that we can, to some extent, do what we want.

Now what is happening at the moment? What is happening is that we know that with technology we can make life easier for human beings; we can make changes. What we are really doing is learning to tinker with the system. But there is very little thinking at the fundamental level as to what sort of people we would like to have. In the long term, that is the question you are bound to come up with.

Do you see what Dr. Crick is saying here? This is the very situation that *Brave New World* said was 600 years away. The question is with us today.

Francis Crick continues:

It's the aim of medical research to try to cure as many diseases as possible, in particular cancer and heart conditions. Those are probably the major killers. But what is going to happen under that situation? What is going to happen essentially is that you can easily work out the age distribution, under a stable population, from the death rate. It means that gradually the population is going to become very old. What medical research is aiming for at the moment is to make the world safe for senility.

Can you see it? Euthanasia becomes thinkable, necessary and "moral." Crick is saying, Let's adjust the humanitarian concept of medicine. Furthermore, Let's begin now. As he says, "It's going to be the people now between fifteen and twenty-five who are going to have to face it, so they may as well start thinking about it now." If this were said by some strange person writing in the Sunday newspaper, perhaps you could laugh it off. But you cannot laugh off Francis Crick!

Crick continues:

We've just seen that the discussion as to how many people there should be in the world has now, as it were, become quite acceptable. It is not acceptable, at the moment, to discuss who should be the parents of the next generation, who should be born, and who should have children. There's a general feeling that if we are all nice to each other and if everybody has 2.3 children, everything will pan out. I don't think that is true. For good genetic reasons, even though you have more medical care, transplantation of organs, and all these things, it would be an unhealthy biological situation. Some group of people should decide some people should have more children and some should have fewer.

. . . You have to decide who is to be born.

Biology is indeed a revolutionary subject when you look at it this way. It is, in fact, *the* major revolutionary subject. It is the one that's going to make the new concepts which will come into social thinking. Biology is not simply, as it were, what you can do with herds of cattle. There are much more intricate things involving people at the psychological level interacting in society, but I don't think you're going to solve all these problems by just tinkering with the genetic material. I think it will turn out that thinking along these lines will have to take place, and if you don't do it in this country, it will start in another country.

Finally, Francis Crick considers where the money for such genetic manipulation is going to come from, and suggests that it be from the government, the state itself. Like John Kenneth Galbraith, Crick believes that it is the intellectuals and especially the academic and scientific world plus the state that will take the initiative.

Crick closes his lecture this way:

This comes to probably the basic thing that I would say. That really what is wanted is education—an education at the level of younger people. It's nice to read articles in *Time* and *Life*, but if you learn something when you're in school, you're forced to learn it in a more regular way. You absorb it, to some extent, at a more impressionable period; you're made to exercise on it. And I think really there should be some thinking if we're to take this new view of looking at man.

Do you see what he is after? He wishes to bring the subject of the biological nature of man and the acceptability of human engineering down into the education even of the lower grades. We had better find out what our children are learning in school!

If man is what Francis Crick says he is, then he is only the product of the impersonal plus time plus chance; he is nothing more than the energy particle extended. And, therefore, he has no intrinsic worth. Our own generation can thus disregard human life. On the one end we will kill the embryo with abortion—anytime anyone wishes—and on the other end we will introduce euthanasia for the old. The one is here and the other is coming.

But where did our sense of man's dignity come from? It came from the Judeo-Christian mentality. For example, we cannot understand idealistic Marxism except as a Christian heresy. Neither the East with its conception of man nor Islam could have produced idealistic Communism. Communism has not won its converts by what Stalin did later (though I think what he did is a natural conclusion to the whole scheme) but rather by the idealistic promises that were made that it would enhance the dignity of man. Materialism never really had a base for this, but it did have a memory to build on.

But with Francis Crick, the concept is gone. We are in the post-Christian world. Man is junk, and man can be treated as junk. If the embryo is in the way, ditch it. If the old person is in the way, ditch him. If you're in the way . . . and that's what lies before us.

The next article appeared in the mass media and is available to everyone. The title is "Taking Life in Our Own Hands: The Test-Tube Baby Is Coming," and it was written by David M. Rorvik and published in *Look* magazine (May 18, 1971). The introduction runs like this:

> "The really revolutionary revolution is to be achieved," Aldous Huxley once wrote, "not in the external world, but in the souls and flesh of human beings." And in his immensely popular and prophetic novel, *Brave New World,* he describes one possible product of such a revolution: a world in which a scientific elite of totalitarian "Predestinators" creates test-tube babies on an assembly line, predetermining in the process their every mental and physical characteristic. It is a world in which everyone is kept high and happy on doctored genes and a drug called "soma." Those who first opened the book in 1932 could at least feel comforted that Huxley placed the revolution 600 years in the future. Now, more than 50 printings later, passages from the book read like paragraphs from our daily newspapers.
>
> The code of life has been cracked, and genetic engineering is on its way. Scientists have husbanded the miracle of conception outside the womb and, it has just been revealed, a living human embryo, created in a test tube from the egg of one woman and the sperm of her husband, has already been transplanted into the uterus of the second woman.

Doctors, specifically Dr. Landrum B. Shettles at Columbia University's College of Physicians and Surgeons, have already removed human eggs, fertilized them and incubated them in the lab. It is now possible to implant a tiny embryo in the womb and create new life. As Rorvik says in this same article,

> ... A completely healthy young woman, reluctant to remove herself from a rewarding career for even a few months, might still produce a child by *hiring* another woman to carry her embryo to term.
>
> Clearly, a new era has dawned. Doctors and scientists around the world are right now preparing to perform these procedures.

In short, the test-tube embryo implant is no longer merely a theory. Even the scientists themselves are aware that great social consequences are at stake. Dr. James D. Watson, the Nobel prize-winning molecular biologist who worked with Francis Crick in breaking the genetic code and describing the DNA template, is concerned. As *Look* magazine says,

> Dr. James D. Watson ... recently warned a congressional subcommittee that "all hell will break loose" in the wake of embryo transplants. "The nature of the bond between parents and children ... and everyone's values about his individual uniqueness," he declared, "could be changed beyond recognition." He urged Congress to establish a commission to consider the ramifications of test-tube conceptions and embryo transplants and possibly even to "take steps quickly" to make them illegal. ...
>
> It was the French biologist, Dr. Jean Rostand, who said that, with the advent of test-tube babies, "it will be little more than a game to change the subject's sex, the color of its eyes, the general proportions of body and limbs, and perhaps the facial features." The "man-farming biologist," he added, might well be tempted to tamper with the intellectual makeup of the subject as well, predetermining, a la Huxley, the behavior and attitudes of an individual for a lifetime.

Here are men who are doing the manipulating and are afraid of what they are doing. Like the scientists who made the hydrogen bomb, the men who really understand are terrorized.

Why do they do it then? Because they live in a universe with only one boundary condition. Christians have two boundary conditions: (1) what men *can* do and (2) what men *should* do. Modern man does not have that latter boundary. Only technology limits him. Modern man does what he can do.

Think back to Eve. Eve had two boundary conditions. She *could* eat the fruit, because it was just some natural food and God had made her with teeth and an esophagus and she could masticate and swallow the fruit. The problem was not technology. The problem was the fact that God had given a second boundary condition: She *shouldn't* do it.

But modern man, standing with only one boundary condition, is filled with terror when he does what he can do, for there is nothing to prevent all of what he sees before him from being done. Men will do these things in the same way that they made the hydrogen bomb. They will build into the genes of a man precisely what they want the man of the future to be.

This indeed is no age to be soft on the Christian view of man!

probing the brain

The cover of the June 21, 1971 issue of *Newsweek* carried a picture of a monkey with electronic censors fastened to his brain; the title of the cover story was "Probing the Brain." You may remember that in *The Church at the End of the 20th Century* (p. 98) I mentioned Dr. José M. R. Delgado who had experimented with censors in the brains of monkeys and in human epileptics. The notice I referred to there was only a small squib that I picked up in the *International Herald Tribune* (May 22, 1970), and to that date it was about the only thing of its nature that I had seen in the mass media. The scientific journals, of course, had been carrying such material, but most of it had not met public attention. A year later *Newsweek* made these scientific developments their cover story. It is a fairly long article (five full pages) and is worth reading in its entirety. It covers the general field of electrical stimulation of the brain or, as it is technically abbreviated, ESB. I will pick up only a few items here.

> The intricate interplay between the neurons of the brain has been compared, depending on the technology of the time, to everything from the shuttles of a loom to the high-speed computer. But the circuits of the brain are infinitely more complex than any of these. "It looks inscrutable," says neurobiologist Stephen Kuffler of Harvard, "only because we don't know the design. Slowly, we're learning more about the design."

Scientists admit that, so far, the brain remains inscrutable. And yet, they insist that tomorrow we will be able to understand it. Even though the computer is not actually comparable to the brain or the brain to the computer, men are working on this basis. Scientists are asking us to bet on their knowledge of tomorrow: Tomorrow and tomorrow and tomorrow our hypotheses will be confirmed.

Francis Crick used this mañana argument in his lecture also. He recognized that there was much yet to learn, but said, "I think that if I had to make a bet, I would put long odds on what I've said: that the whole biological world evolves essentially by chance within the framework of the possible and is not pre-programmed." Obviously such arguments rest on faith, not on science.   **27**

What, therefore, really makes man tick? Freud, while he was primarily a psychological determinist, thought that the workings of the mind and the emotions might eventually be found to be chemically determined. Before him, of course, the Marquis de Sade was truly a chemical determinist in a philosophic sense. De Sade's books alternate between pornography and philosophy. The former provides the excitement, the vehicle to get across the philosophic concept. His point was very simple and yet very profound: Nature has made the male stronger than the female, and therefore it is right for the man to do anything he wants to the woman. This is the basis of sadism. In other words, in a deterministic system, whatever is is right. Once one accepts the presuppositions of determinism, whether chemical or psychological, values and morals disappear. All that remain are sociological, arbitrary absolutes.

Many of today's scientists are persuaded that the source of man's hungers, drives and needs lies totally in the brain's circuits—in the mechanism of man. We are not far from de Sade here.

Near the end of the *Newsweek* article on ESB, we find the speculation that someday we may be able to take a pill that will help us learn French more easily. Scientists at the moment generally debunk this notion, and yet:

> French pills or no French pills, the fact remains that the day may come when the combined efforts of the brain researchers and the genetic engineers will enable men to alter radically the functioning of the human mind, and while some scientists and philosophers take cheer in the prospect, others find it a somber one, indeed. Yale's Delgado, for instance, foresees a future society that has become "psycho-civilized" through the

application of ESB and other techniques. Psychologist-philosopher Arthur Koestler argues that the psycho-civilizing process can begin none too soon if man is to be saved from himself.

It was Arthur Koestler who wrote *The Ghost in the Machine* and who suggested the possibility of putting chemicals in the drinking water in order to bring the parts of each man's brain together so that he would be more peaceful (*Horizon,* Spring 1968, p. 43). *Newsweek* continues:

"It's a race against the clock," says Koestler. He specifically advocates biochemical manipulation to insure the dominance of the brain's rational cortex over the irrational, animal-like "old cortex." Koestler asks, "Why despair of the possibility of stabilizing people, of harmonizing them without really castrating them, without sterilizing them mentally?"

Others take a distinctly gloomy view of the prospects of the future. The question is asked: if human behavior can really be so radically altered by psychosurgery, ESB, biofeedback and genetic tinkering, does it not follow that society itself might someday be governed by the wholly rational supermen with their superbrains whom the brain researchers and their colleagues have created?

Here is C. S. Lewis's *That Hideous Strength* with a vengeance. I strongly urge Christians to read carefully this prophetic piece of science fiction. For what Lewis casts in fantasy and science fiction is with us not tomorrow but today.

The *Newsweek* article goes on to comment on the possibility that such supermen will be developed:

. . . not many really foresee the emergence of any such sad new world as the pessimists envisage. . . . At Johns

Hopkins, biophysicist Marcus Jacobson puts both the problem and the solution a bit differently. "We need to ask whether or not we really want supermen with superbrains," he says. Jacobson thinks that man is served well enough by the brain he now carries. "It is a perfect instrument," he adds. "It can take man wherever we might want it to take us."

Jacobson is right. While we would add that man is more than a brain, our brain is a good brain. God made the human brain. But the fact is that man is fooling with it. Electrical stimulation of the brain, genetic engineering, chemicals in the drinking water—the human brain will be drastically changed.

ice-cube babies

Newsweek (July 12, 1971) brings us one step further—ice-cube babies:

More than one genetic engineer has seriously suggested that the semen of great men should be frozen and stored. In this way, the argument goes, their outstanding endowments could be readily melded to those of superior women for the enrichment of mankind.

Isn't that what Plato said in relation to the philosopher kings? But Plato didn't have the tools. We have.

Though many social and ethical objections might be raised against this kind of eugenic scheme, a Los Angeles physician has now shown that pregnancy by means of frozen semen is at last scientifically feasible—and has used artificial insemination with deep-freeze sperm to help nearly 70 women have babies.

Since we have the tools, we are using them. Frozen-sperm banks are springing up all over the United States. You pay so much for the initial storing of the semen, and then so much a month. The article focuses on the work of Dr. Edward T. Tyler of the Tyler Clinic:

A number of husbands have had semen samples frozen

and stored at Tyler's clinic before undergoing vasectomy procedures. . . . With the number of vasectomies rising steadily, Tyler plans to open an entire bank at his clinic for this purpose. Tyler points out that frozen storage of semen is useful for husbands who travel a lot.

These things may sound like Buck Rogers, but they are going on now. It's the world we are living in. It's the world we are raising our children in. It's the world the church has to face and we had better face it openly and understandingly. We must not weaken the absolutes God has given us propositionally in Scripture.

Time (September 20, 1971) carried this story as its lead item:

kenneth
clark:
a
pill
for
peace

> Dr. Kenneth Clark, President of the American Psychological Association, has proposed a startling cure for international aggression. The world's leaders, he told the A.P.A. meeting in Washington, should be required to take "psychotechnological medication"—pills or other treatments to curb their aggressive behavior and induce them to govern more humanely. Such a pharmacological fix, Clark argued, "would provide the masses with the security that their leaders would not or could not sacrifice them on the altars of the leaders' personal ego pathos."

But, as *Time* points out, the question arises: Who is going to dispense the pills? Who polices the police? Who is going to sit on top of the power pile and dispense the drugs? If they were voluntary, those who were most in need of them would be precisely those who would not take them. If they could somehow be made compulsory, then the dispensers would become the dominators. In the speech itself (*Intellectual Digest*, February 1972) Clark says, "The Era of Psychotechnology . . . cannot now be avoided. It must be used affirmatively, wisely and with compassion." Who is to be trusted to use such power? Notice that Dr. Clark's suggestion is almost identical to Koestler's in *The Ghost in the Machine*.

skinner: beyond freedom and dignity

We turn, finally, to a book by and a series of articles about B. F. Skinner. His recent *Beyond Freedom and Dignity* undoubtedly will be one of the most important books for discussion in intellectual circles in the next several years. It was released in the fall of 1971, but just prior to its release it was published in *Psychology Today* (August 1971) in an extensive though abbreviated form. Many subsequent articles have appeared, perhaps the most impressive of which is *Time*'s cover story (September 20, 1971). The introduction to B. F. Skinner by T. George Harris, "All the World's a Box," in *Psychology Today*'s August issue should also be singled out for special attention.

B. F. Skinner's *Beyond Freedom and Dignity* is not a new thing in the intellectual world. Skinner himself has written previous books, the most popular being *Walden Two*, a science fiction novel in which Skinner envisions a utopian commune based on behavioristic principles. Since 1948, when *Walden Two* was published, Skinner's behaviorist ideas have been receiving a large audience and a good deal of controversy has raged around the concepts of behaviorism itself. In a way, it was once relatively easy to dismiss the ideas because they were given a novelistic presentation. Now, however, *Beyond Freedom and Dignity* makes explicit and direct, and claims scientific objectivity for, the conceptions which were given such graphic representation in the novel.

What, then, is this behavioristic psychology which has caused such a furor? Essentially, behaviorism declares that all of a person's behavior is the result of environmental conditioning, whether that conditioning occurred prior to birth and resides in the genes or subsequent to birth and resides in the external environment. As Skinner says, "Personal exemption from a complete determinism is revoked as scientific analysis progresses, particularly in accounting for the behavior of the individual" (*Beyond Freedom and Dignity,* p. 21). That is, all of an individual's actions are either predetermined by his heredity or immediately determined by his surroundings. In any case, there is nothing in man, no "ego" or central core of personality, which is not linked to the pre-determined causal chain of events.

Skinner says that up till now almost all of humanity has considered man to be in some sense autonomous, that is, that there is in each individual an "ego" or mind or center of consciousness which can freely choose one or another course of action. But, Skinner says, autonomous man does not exist, and it is the task of behavioral psychology to abolish the conception.

As Skinner puts it,

What is being abolished is autonomous man—the inner man, the homunculus man, the possessing demon, the man defended by the literatures of freedom and dignity.

His abolition has long been overdue. Autonomous man is a device used to explain what we cannot explain in any other way. He has been constructed from our ignorance, and as our understanding increases, the very stuff of which he is composed vanishes. Science does not dehumanize man, it de-homunculizes him, and it must do so if it is to prevent the abolition of the human species. To man *qua* man we readily say good riddance. Only by dispossessing him can we turn to the real causes of human behavior. Only then can we turn from the inferred to the observed, from the miraculous to the natural, from the inaccessible to the manipulable. (pp. 200-201)

It is important to understand what Skinner means by *autonomous man*. We must distinguish it from the concept of autonomous man I have described in *Escape from Reason* and *The God Who Is There*. I have used the phrase to describe the person who tries to divorce himself from God, who attempts to set up his own autonomy and his own dignity on his own basis, who tries to make man as man the measure of all things. But this is not what Skinner means. By *autonomous man* he means the notion that man is not a part of the cosmic machine, that something in man stands in contrast to the cosmic machine and allows man to make real choices. This is just the sort of man which Christians must affirm as being there if man is to retain his sense of worth and to have the value the Bible and the Christian culture which came from the biblical base ascribe to man. In other words, Christians affirm the autonomy of man in Skinner's sense.

Skinner, on the other hand, declares that man is not autonomous in this sense, not separate from his surrounding environment. Everything man is, everything man makes, everything man thinks is completely, one hundred percent, determined by his environment. After the publication of *Beyond Freedom and Dignity* when he was at the Center for the Study of Democratic Institutions, he spoke at Westmont College in Santa Barbara, California. There he said, "The individual does not initiate anything." In fact, he said that any time man is freed from one kind of control, he merely comes under another kind of control.

Christians consider that man is autonomous in that he

is significant, he affects the environment. In behavioristic psychology, the situation is reversed. All behavior is determined not from within but from without. Notice this: "You" don't exist. Man is not there. All that is there is a bundle of conditioning, a collection of what you have been in the past: your genetic makeup and your environment. But Skinner goes a step further, subordinates the genetic factor, and suggests that man's behavior can be almost totally controlled by controlling the environment. Some behaviorists would differ with him on this last point.

How is it that the environment controls behavior? Here Skinner brings up the concept of "operant conditioning." This notion is based on his work with pigeons and rats. The basic idea is that "when a bit of behavior is followed by a certain consequence, it is more likely to occur again, and a consequence having this effect is called a reinforcer" (p. 27). That is, for example, "anything the organism does that is followed by the receipt of food is more likely to be done again whenever the organism is hungry" (p. 27). There are two kinds of reinforcers, negative reinforcers which have aversive effects and positive reinforcers whose effect is positive. Skinner contends that only the positive reinforcers should be used. In other words, in order to reinforce a certain kind of behavior, one should not punish; he should reward. If a person is surrounded by an atmosphere in which he gets a sufficient reward for doing what society would like him to do, he will automatically do this without ever knowing why he is doing it.

Skinner insists that all of our action is like this, that none of it (whether consciously controlled by someone or simply controlled by the haphazardness of what happens around us) is determined by an individual personally. Skinner says, "The apparent freedom respected by weak measures [of control] is merely inconspicuous control" (p. 97). Speaking more to the political issue, he says, "A permissive government is government that leaves control to other sources" (p. 97). There is, therefore, no place for anything specifically personal or human or autonomous. Not only does man have no soul, he has no mind; he neither initiates, originates nor creates. This makes Michelangelo's painting on the ceiling of the Sistine Chapel purely the result of conditioning. Not only morals but every vestige of everything that makes human life valuable from the standpoint of what God meant us to be as men in his image is eradicated.

christianity and conditioning

It is important at this point to recognize what the Christian position is. The Christian does not say that there is *no* chemical or psychological conditioning. Some may argue that way, but they are trapped because chemical and psychological conditioning can be demonstrated. My height was determined at conception by the chemical properties of my genes. Many aspects of my physical makeup were conditioned by heredity. But to a Christian, though man may undergo a good deal of conditioning, he is not only the product of conditioning. Man has a mind; he exists as an ego, an entity standing over against the machine-like part of his being.

But Skinner rejects this Christian view, and, in fact, he rejected Christianity itself a long time ago. T. George Harris comments:

His family was warm and stable, and much concerned about behavior. "I was taught to fear God, the police, and what people will think," he recalls, and he suspects that his reaction may have led him to try proving that people don't think at all. An old-maid school teacher taught him English composition in the public school and Old Testament language and morals in the Presbyterian Sunday school. His father took him through the county jail to show him the punishment he would face if he were to develop a criminal mind. He was never whipped. Once when he used a bad word, his mother washed out his mouth with soap. Grandmother Skinner had him peer into the glowing coals of the parlor stove to gain a sense of hell.

According to Skinner himself, then, that's the kind of Christianity he was taught. So let's take note: When Christians and evangelical churches do not have the courage (regardless of what others think) to stress the balance of the exhibition of the love of God and the holiness of God and to make an absolute distinction between cultural norms and biblical absolutes, a whole generation is being opened to the possibility of taking Skinner's kind of action—rejecting Christ himself. We will destroy the church if we do not have the courage in a radical day like ours to hold onto the absolutes of the Word of God regardless of the cost. But also when we train children to take equally what the Bible says and what people will think, we destroy the Bible's authority when the chips are down in the university. Cry for Skinner. But cry for a whole generation often raised the same way!

Skinner himself recognizes very well the implications of his behaviorism. For example, he recognizes that within behavioral terms democracy is essentially impossible. Since all behavior is controlled by the environment, it is possible to manipulate the environment so as to produce the kind of behavior one wants. For Skinner a democracy is controlled by the concept of autonomous man, a false concept. Far more effective control can be wielded by those who recognize and utilize the tenets of behavioral psychology. In the Santa Barbara interview he said that he wants university students to know how to control better if they are to be in teaching or politics. As Skinner puts it in his book, "The problem is to induce people not to be good but to behave well" (p. 67). Furthermore, "It is the environment which is 'responsible' for the objectionable behavior, and it is the environment, not some attribute of the individual, which must be changed" (p. 74).

The obvious question which arises at this point is, Who is going to do the controlling? Who will determine what proper behavior is? As *Time* puts it:

> The ultimate logical dilemma in Skinner's thinking is this: What are the sources of the standards of good and evil in his ideal society? Indeed, who decides even what constitutes pleasure or pain, reward or punishment, when man and his environment can be limitlessly manipulated? Skinner himself believes in Judeo-Christian ethics combined with the scientific tradition. But he fails to answer how it is possible to accept those ethics without also accepting something like the "inner person" with an autonomous conscience. (p. 53)

Skinner insists that men of good will must adopt more effective techniques, using them for good purposes to keep despots from using them for bad purposes. But what does that mean in a setting such as this? Where are these good people going to come from? Who do we find when we get inside of the man with a white lab coat? We find a faulty, lost man, don't we? Where are these great benevolent manipulators going to come from? Talk about utopia! This is the most utopian concept of all. Skinner's utopianism keeps showing through when he is pressed in discussion. In the British Broadcasting Corporation's *The Listener* (September 30, 1971) he says, "We must hope that a culture will emerge in which those who have power will use it for the general good. . . . If the power of a technology of behaviour does indeed fall into the hands of despots, it will be because it has been rejected by men and women of good will." In the behavioristic scheme that sentence is as meaningless as when he said in the Santa Barbara interview that he *accepts* the control of those who pay him. Has Skinner himself found some magic way to be able to *accept* or *reject* beyond conditioning? Although he does not know it, he is here speaking as a man made in the image of God.

Skinner himself in his practice functions on the basis of the values of the Judeo-Christian ethic because he lives in the memory of the Christian position. But what happens when people no longer have this memory? The only way Skinner can live with his own position is to cheat and hang onto the Christian values even when he has supposedly given them up.

When Skinner is consistent, the valuelessness of his values becomes obvious. For example, in defining good he says, "Good things are positive reinforcers" (p. 103). Or again: "Things are good (positively reinforcing) or bad (negatively reinforcing) presumably because of the contingencies of survival under which the species evolved" (p. 104). Along the same line he comments on the Christian notion of heaven from the behaviorist standpoint: "Heaven is portrayed as a collection of positive reinforcers and hell is a collection of negative, although they are contingent upon behavior executed *before death.* (Personal survival value after death may be a metaphorical adumbration of the evolutionary concept of survival value)" (p. 136). Ultimately, he is reduced to saying that survival—the biological continuity of the human *race*—is the only value in the universe: "Survival is the only value according to which a culture is eventually to be judged, and any practice that furthers survival has survival value by definition" (p. 136). This was also Bertrand Russell's view at the end of his life. The reason he spoke out so strongly against the hydrogen bomb was that he was afraid there would soon be no one left to look at a sunset. In reality men with a naturalistic presupposition have nowhere else to go for values. I was impressed again with this recently when George Wald of Harvard and I were lecturers at a conference in Acapulco, Mexico. After a brilliant presentation of naturalism, he also presented the continuity of the race as his one value generated out of his world of chance. Skinner summed it up in the Santa Barbara interview with the sentence, "All values derive from survival value."

When Skinner, however, asks himself why he or any man should be concerned about the survival of a particular kind of culture, he says that the only honest answer is this: "There is no good reason why you should be concerned, but if your culture has not convinced you that there is, so much the worse for your culture" (p. 137). Skinner does not seem to notice that he has gotten himself into a logical box. Ultimately, what he is saying reduces to whatever is is right, and, if whatever is is right, then there is no value over against which one can judge anything as good or bad. If it is, it is good. And if everything that is is good, then any concept of bad is either illogical or trivial. Neither a man like Skinner nor a man like George Wald has any reason why the survival of the race is desirable.

Within the Skinnerian system there are no ethical controls. There is no boundary limit to what can be done by the elite in whose hands control resides. This is precisely the sort of thing we find in John Kenneth Gal-

braith's establishment elite in *The New Industrial State.*
And we find more and more swing to this direction in
the publications of the new "liberal mind."

The reduction of man's value to zero is really one of
the important factors which triggered the student rebellion at Berkeley and elsewhere. Those students sensed
that they were being turned into zeros and they re-
volted. Christians should have sensed it long before and
said and exhibited that we have an alternative. The fact
is that Christianity has a base on which a realistic and
humane democracy, a far-reaching freedom with a form,
was built and can be built again.

Democracy, freedom without chaos, as we know it in
northern Europe was built on the Reformation and it
has not existed anywhere else, except perhaps for a very
few years in very small city states in Greece long ago.
This cannot be built or last long without the position
outlined in Samuel Rutherford's *Rex Lex.* When one
removes both the Bible in which God has spoken propositionally and the resulting Christian consensus, freedom
without chaos will not long remain. It can't. Something
will take its place, and it will be one of the elites.

T. George Harris summarizes it this way:

But man in his conceit refuses to accept himself as an
organism shaped by his environment. The trouble
starts, Skinner says, with the proud belief that under-
lies democracy: the notion that in each of us there is a
mentalistic being—an ego, personality, anima, spirit,
character, soul or mind—that is somehow free.

He denies the existence of this Autonomous Man
and of any other cognitive entity able to claim, as
Americans did in the Declaration of Independence, to
hold "unalienable rights." In cold passion, Skinner
seeks to destroy our pretentions to the freedom and

dignity whose literature is written in brave blood.

To take their place, Skinner offers the passionless hypothesis of his experimental laboratory: each man and woman is a unique bundle of behaviors determined by environment; only that, and nothing more. Through evolution the environment selected the behaviors that survive in our genes, and environmental conditioning shapes each of us in this life. If you would control, or change, human behavior, you need only control environment. (*Psychology Today,* August 1971, p. 33)

Surely, we say, what Skinner suggests could never be put into practice. But listen to what Harris says: "Nobody would panic at Skinner's attack upon our idea of freedom if he were only talking. But he has a program, and followers to push it. In more than 40 years of psychological research, he has developed and proved out ingenious techniques for the radical modification of behavior, animal or human, by operant conditioning."

Everywhere I go I find behaviorists completely committed to his view. Man is accepted as a machine, and he is treated as a machine. Such professionals are there by the hundreds, some of them with understanding, some of them with power, some of them only in little places. In some places they control the educational process down into the earliest days of school. A question may be asked: Aren't pattern drills in the language lab always behavioristic, and even when these are helpful don't they support Harris's warning that Skinner must be taken seriously because "he has a program and followers to push it"? A brilliant young girl teaching psychology in a social science department in a British university was forced to choose whether to teach on a behavioristic level or to leave the university. The girl walked out. She had to. Behaviorism is not something that we can simply dismiss. Its power is too great.

To make his case, Skinner often resorts to using heavily connotative language. For example, he tells us that modern physics and biology no longer attribute the behavior of things to personified causes such as essences, qualities or natures. But, he says, "Almost everyone who is concerned with human affairs—as political scientist, philosopher, man of letters, economist, psychologist, linguist, sociologist, theologian, anthropologist, educator, or psychotherapist—continues to talk about human behavior in this *prescientific* way" (p. 9, italics mine; see also p. 101). His way, of course, is the *scientific* way. And what is the scientific way? He puts it in the negative first:

> We are told [by those who are prescientific] that to control the number of people in the world we need to change *attitudes* toward children, overcome *pride* in size of family or in sexual potency, build some sense of *responsibility* toward offspring, and reduce the role played by a large family in allaying *concern* for old age. (pp. 9-10)

Skinner says none of these things exist. There are no *attitudes.* There is no *pride.* There is no sense of *responsibility.* All of this is mere conditioning. That's the scientific way of looking at man. "Man is a machine in the sense that he is a complex system behaving in lawful ways, but the complexity is extraordinary" (p. 202). In Santa Barbara he said all our feelings are a result of our acts, and we act as we do because of our previous history.

In response to Joseph Wood Krutch who has argued that Hamlet's exclamation "How like a god!" is closer to the truth, Skinner says, "Pavlov, the behavioral scientist, emphasized 'How like a dog!' But that was a step forward. A god is the archetypal pattern of an explanatory

how like a dog!

43

fiction, of a miracle-working mind, of the metaphysical man. Man is much more than a dog, but like a dog he is within the range of scientific analysis" (p. 201).

Man is dead. And with him dies the whole of Western culture and all of its literature and art. Chapters two and three of his book are dedicated to attacking what he calls literatures of freedom and dignity. This literature has taught men that they make choices, that they have dignity. So Skinner's war is not simply against Christians; it is against anyone who thinks that there is such a thing as a mind and anyone who writes concerning the freedom and dignity of man. Such men have become the enemy and they must be wiped out or at least removed from places of influence. Again in the Santa Barbara interview, he said that something needs to be done about the commitment to freedom we have had.

We are on the verge of the largest revolution the world has ever seen—the control and shaping of men through genetic engineering and chemical and psychological conditioning. Will people accept it? I don't think they would accept it if (1) they had not already been taught to accept the presuppositions that lead to it and (2) they were not in such despair. But many have accepted the presuppositions and they are in despair. Many of our secular schools have consistently taught these presuppositions, and unhappily many of our Christian lower schools and colleges have taught the crucial subjects no differently than the secular schools.[1]

No one directly changes his mind, says Skinner. Think how shocking this would have sounded to us only a few years ago. There is no such thing as changing one's mind, because there is no mind. So when you say, "I changed my mind," or "I will cause my child to change his mind," or "I will ask someone to accept Christ as his

Savior"—all these are nonsense words. No one directly changes anyone's mind. By manipulating environmental contingencies, one makes changes that are said to indicate a change of mind, but it's an illusion.

The way Skinner treats his critics and anyone who would disagree with him is especially interesting. He writes, "A literature of freedom may inspire a sufficiently fanatical opposition to controlling practices to generate a neurotic if not psychotic response. There are signs of emotional instability in those who have been deeply affected by the literature." Anyone who would stand against B. F. Skinner is neurotic or psychotic. This accusation is immediately reminiscent of Ward 7 in Russia, the wing in the mental hospital full of men with deviant political views. A person can be put in Ward 7 without a trial and without a sentence. As long as the state says he is insane, he remains there. What Skinner is saying is, If you stand against my position you are really neurotic or emotionally unstable. Then he names some well-known men who differ with him (Fyodor Dostoevsky, Arthur Koestler and Peter Gay), accusing them of namecalling (p. 165)!

Skinner is out to attack or undercut all who say that intentionally designing culture is an unwarranted meddling in the basic rights of man. As he says, "Life, liberty, and the pursuit of happiness are basic rights. But they are the rights of the individual and were listed as such at a time when the literatures of freedom and dignity were concerned with the aggrandizement of the individual. They have only a minor bearing on the survival of a culture" (p. 180). All such ideas are passé. Twice Skinner specifically attacks C. S. Lewis. Why? Because he is a Christian and writes in the tradition of the literatures of freedom and dignity. You will notice that he does not attack the evangelical church, probably because he doesn't think it's a threat. Unhappily, he is largely right about this. Many of us are too sleepy to be a threat in the battle of tomorrow. But he understands that a man like C. S. Lewis who writes literature that stirs men is indeed a threat. So he turns on Lewis (pp. 200 and 206) at exactly this point.

Finally, we reach Skinner's conclusion. After saying good riddance to man as man, after destroying any concept of autonomous man and after reducing man to a mere machine, he winds up his book with one of the most utopian statements I have ever read:

It is hard to imagine a world in which people live together without quarreling, maintain themselves by producing the food, shelter, and clothing they need, enjoy themselves and contribute to the enjoyment of others in art, music, literature and games, consume only a reasonable part of the resources of the world and add as little as possible to its pollution, bear no more children than can be raised decently, continue to explore the world around them and discover better ways of dealing with it, and come to know themselves accurately and, therefore, manage themselves effectively. Yet all this is possible, and even the slightest sign of progress should bring a kind of change which in traditional terms would be said to assuage wounded vanity, offset a sense of hopelessness or nostalgia, correct the impression that "we neither can nor need to do anything for ourselves," and promote a "sense of freedom and dignity" by building "a sense of confidence and worth." In other words, it should abundantly reinforce those who have been induced by their culture to work for its survival. . . . We have not yet seen what man can make of man. (pp. 214—215)

46

How utopian can you be? We thought the drug people were utopian when they said, Put LSD in the drinking water, everybody will be turned on and our society's problems will be solved! But don't believe Skinner's unbased utopianism—it's the death of man.

To accept Skinner's utopia is to launch out completely on faith. It leaves us with four unanswerable questions: (1) Who is going to control the controllers? (2) Where is the second boundary condition that puts a limit of "right" or "wrong" to the first boundary condition of what man can do to man technologically? (3) Why does the biological continuity of the human race have any value at all? (4) If man is such a poor observer as to so wrongly observe himself for 40,000 or so years (accepting for the moment the modern dating systems of science) and consistently conclude that man is different from non-man, then how can we trust man's observation of anything? If we follow Skinner, we are left with a total scepticism in regard to all knowledge and knowing. Further, if the only way man *is able to* function in either knowledge or values is as Skinner does by acting on the basis of that which he and his system destroy, are we not left with Skinner himself as a pitiful man—not as a rat or pigeon pushing levers but as a poor, optimistic rat or pigeon pushing levers?

What do we and our children face? The **conclusion** biological bomb, genetic engineering, chemical engineering, electrical stimulation of the brain, the behavioristic manipulation of man. All these have come to popular attention only very recently. But they are not twenty years away. They are not five years away. They are here now in technological breakthroughs and soon in practice. This is where we live, and as true Christians we must be ready. This is no time for weakness in the church of Christ.

What has happened to man? We must see him as one who has torn himself away both from the infinite-personal God who created him as finite but in his image, and from God's revelation to him. Made in God's image, man was made to be great, he was made to be beautiful and he was made to be creative in life and art. But his rebellion has led him into making himself into nothing but a machine.

Note

[1] *In recent months Stanley Kubrick's* A Clockwork Orange *has intensified these issues through the cinema and has prepared an even larger number of people to think about the technological possibilities and to raise the question of conditioned manipulation as acceptable in the light of the increasing social chaos.*